ANCIENT EGYPT

FARMING & FOOD

Jane Shuter

Heinemann Library
Des Plaines, Illinois

Designed by Clare Sleven
Illustrations by Jonathan Adams, Jeff Edwards
Printed in Hong Kong

03 02 01 00 99
10 9 8 7 6 5 4 3 2

Library of Congress Cataloging-in-Publication Data

Shuter, Jane.
    Farming and food / Jane Shuter.
        p.   cm. -- (Ancient Egypt)
    Includes bibliographical references (p.) and index.
    Summary: An introduction to farming in ancient Egypt, including the cycles of the farming year, irrigation and flooding of the Nile, land ownership, and typical foods.
    ISBN 1-57572-730-7 (lib. bdg.)
    1. Agriculture--Egypt--History--Juvenile literature. 2. Food habits--Egypt--History--Juvenile literature. 3. Egypt--Civilization--To 332 B.C.--Juvenile literature.   [1. Agriculture--Egypt--History. 2. Food habits--Egypt--History. 3. Egypt--Civilization--To 332 B.C.] I. Title. II. Series: Shuter, Jane. Ancient Egypt.
    S427.S48   1998
    630'.932--dc21   98-11750
                                                                            CIP
                                                                            AC

Acknowledgments
The Publishers would like to thank the following for permission to reproduce photographs: British Museum: pp. 8, 10–11, 28, 29; Michael Holford: p. 16; Middle East Pictures: C. Osborne p. 5; Photo Archiv: J. Leipe pp. 13, 20, 21; Werner Forman Archive: pp. 9, 17, 23, 25

Cover photograph reproduced with permission of Jurgen Liepe, Photo-Archive

Every effort has been made to contact copyright holders of any material reproduced in this book. Any omissions will be rectified in subsequent printings if notice is given to the Publisher.

Any words appearing in the text in bold, **like this**, are explained in the Glossary.

CONTENTS

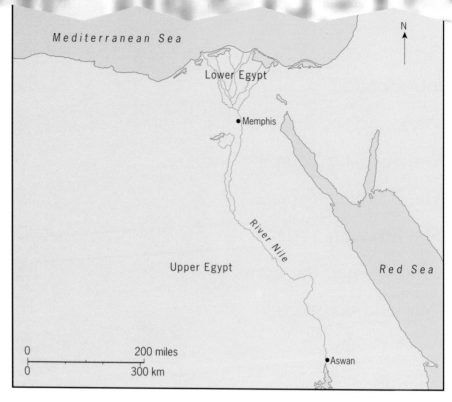

Map showing the Nile River running through Egypt, with the Mediterranean Sea to the north, Lower Egypt, Memphis, Upper Egypt, Aswan, and the Red Sea. Scale: 200 miles / 300 km. N (north arrow).

THE NILE RIVER

The Nile River runs the whole length of Egypt. In ancient times, it flooded each year. When the water went back down, a thick layer of mud was left covering the land that had been flooded. Farmers could grow **crops** on this, but the rest of the land was too dry. They had to fit farming in around the flood (**inundation**). During the inundation, they did other jobs.

This chart shows different stages in the long history of Ancient Egypt. The red blocks show when pharaohs were weak and no one ran the whole country.

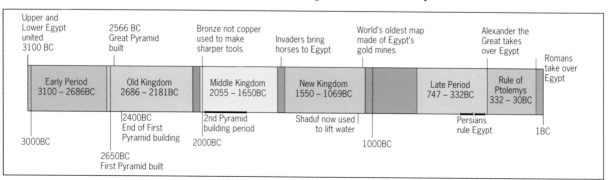

Timeline chart:

Upper and Lower Egypt united 3100 BC

2566 BC Great Pyramid built

Bronze not copper used to make sharper tools

Invaders bring horses to Egypt

World's oldest map made of Egypt's gold mines

Alexander the Great takes over Egypt

Romans take over Egypt

| Early Period 3100 – 2686BC | Old Kingdom 2686 – 2181BC | Middle Kingdom 2055 – 1650BC | New Kingdom 1550 – 1069BC | | Late Period 747 – 332BC | Rule of Ptolemys 332 – 30BC |

2400BC End of First Pyramid building

2nd Pyramid building period

Shaduf now used to lift water

Persians rule Egypt

3000BC

2650BC First Pyramid built

2000BC

1000BC

1BC

THE FARMING YEAR

There were three stages in the farming year. The inundation lasted from July to October. November to April was the planting and growing time. May to June was the **harvest** time.

MEASURING THE FLOOD

It was important to know how much the river would flood each year. Walled steps were built down to the river. Marks were carved on the walls at the same time every year. (You can still see these marks today.) **Scribes** used these measures (called Nilometers) to predict how much the river would probably flood. The river usually rose by 26 to 33 feet (8 to 10 meters) at Aswan and 20 to 26 feet (6 to 8 meters) at Memphis.

Farmers still farm along the edges of the Nile River today. Now a dam has been built to stop the yearly flooding.

Most of Ancient Egypt was **desert**. It was hot and dry all year round. It hardly ever rained. Farmers had to water their **crops** every day.

During most of the Ancient Egyptian period, people lifted water from the river one bucket at a time. Then they carried it to the fields. From earliest times, farmers tried to keep as much of the water from the **inundation** as possible.

KEEPING BACK THE WATER

Farmers made big ponds to hold the flood water. **Ditches** ran from the ponds to the fields and around them. Wooden **sluices** divided the ditches. When the sluice boards were pulled up, the water came out. When they were closed, the water was held back. Farmers could let out as much water as they needed to water their fields.

Every year people cleared weeds and mud out of the ditches and ponds before the inundation. They had to work fast. Many people helped as part of their **corvée**—work they had to do for the **pharaoh**.

When the flood waters began to go down in late October, government **scribes** measured the fields. They marked each plot of land with stones. Then the farmers could begin to work. They turned over the thick mud with wooden **plows**, which were often pulled by **oxen**. Then the scribes gave out the **grain** to sow. They prayed to the gods for a good **harvest**. The seeds were sown and animals were driven over the soil to tread the seeds into it.

A tomb model of a farmer plowing. Models like this were buried with people, along with all the other things they needed for their next life.

Farmers sowed seeds by hand from baskets. In this picture, the mud is hard. Farmers break it up before the seeds are sown.

AN EASY LIFE?

Ancient Egyptian **tomb paintings** show tomb owners farming in their best clothes. These paintings had to show a perfect world. They wanted the dead to go to a perfect place, so this is what they showed. In real life, farming was hard work.

SOME WRITINGS FROM ANCIENT EGYPT TELL US ABOUT FARMERS. IN ABOUT 2000 B.C., A SCRIBE WROTE:

The farmer is dressed in rags and worn out from standing in mud. By the time he has walked home at the end of the day, he is exhausted. [*Some tomb paintings show farmers talking as they work. This is an example from the wall of a tomb:*] Go on, guide it! Hurry, hurry with the oxen! Mind your feet. Watch out. The master's there and he's watching us!

In March, people **harvested** the **grain**. Men, women, and children flocked to the fields when the grain was ripe. It was cut down, sorted, and stored. Then there was just time to grow a **crop** of beans or other vegetables before the **inundation**.

KEEPING COUNT

It was important to have enough grain to feed everyone for a whole year, so the **pharaoh's scribes** organized the harvest. They figured how much grain should come from each field. They checked how much was actually cut. Then they took a share for the pharaoh's **granaries**.

A copy of a **tomb painting** showing harvest time. The scribes are carefully recording everything.

BAD YEARS

When the Nile River had a "low year," there was less mud left behind to grow crops. Then there was not enough grain to feed everyone. Pharaohs had to buy grain from other countries to make sure that everyone was fed. Despite this, many people died of **starvation** in bad years.

In about 2000 B.C., a priest, Heqanakhte, was sent north from Thebes on business for the pharaoh. He wrote to his family:

Is the Nile very low this year? It seems to be here. I have collected as much food for you as I can. But it is not much, for there is not much to get. Almost everyone is looking for food.

During the **inundation**, all of the farmland was under water. Farmers spent the time mending tools and caring for the animals. If they worked on land belonging to a **temple** or the **pharaoh**, they were given other jobs to do. Usually, many people were needed to help build.

HAPY, GOD OF THE NILE

Hapy was the god who controlled the Nile River. Ancient Egyptians prayed to him for a good inundation. A low inundation could mean **starvation** for many of the poorest people. A high inundation was bad too—homes would be flooded. A low flood was feared the most as this prayer to Hapy shows (it was written in about 1800 B.C.):

Lord of the fish, he sends the wild birds south as he rises. He is father to the barley and wheat. If he is slow to rise, then people hold their breath, grow fierce as food grows short. When he rises well, the people and the land rejoice.

A **tomb model** showing fishing boats. The boats were made from bundles of reeds tied together. There are tiny model fish in the net hung between the boats.

These fishermen have already caught some fish.

The fishermen use paddles to steer and move the boats along.

The boats were made from bundles of redds tied together.

These are tiny model fish in the net slung between the boats.

The **pharaoh** owned all of the land in Ancient Egypt. But he did not run it all by himself. Most of the land was divided into **estates**. These estates were different shapes and sizes and were run by different people. Most of the farmers worked on the estates.

ESTATES

The biggest estates gave everything they made or grew to the pharaoh or important **temples**. The pharaoh's lands were run by important families who often had smaller estates of their own. They kept most of the **crops** from their estates (they had to give some to the pharaoh as a **tax**). They passed their estates on to their children. But the pharaoh could take their estates away from them at any time. He could also take the **grain** from their granaries to feed people when grain was scarce.

An Ancient Egyptian estate. The family that ran the estate would have lived in the large central building surrounded by storerooms and room for the servants.

Historians today are not sure if Ancient Egyptian farmers rented the land they farmed. They may have farmed the land in return for a home and part of the **crops**. We do know that they all worked on **estates**, although some farmers seem to have taken on extra land to farm for themselves.

A PIECE OF LAND

Farmland was divided into pieces called **aruras**. Each arura grew enough food to feed a family for a year. Most farmers farmed one arura for the estate. Some families farmed spare land for themselves. The crops from any extra land they farmed were theirs to keep or sell after they had given part of them as **tax**.

Farmers had only wooden tools to work with during most of the Ancient Egyptian period.

hand **plow**

These scoops were used to shake off the outside layer of the grain.

FLOOD TIME

We do not know exactly what all farmers did during the **inundation**. Workers on big estates owned by **temples** or the **pharaoh** did building work for their masters. Many farmers on smaller estates did other work on the estate. Some farmers may have had a second job, such as making baskets, which they did during this time.

The Ancient Egyptians had no machinery and very few labor-saving tools. All building jobs needed many people to move huge stones or sculptures, like the one in this picture, to the right places.

FOOD: GRAIN

The most important food and drink in Ancient Egypt were bread and beer. Both were made from **grain**—barley or emmer (a type of wheat). So it was important to grow a lot of grain and store it carefully.

BREAD
There were many types and shapes of bread made with flour from different mixes of grain. The flour was made by crushing the grain and shaking off the outside husks. The grain was then ground between two stones. The flour had bits of stone in it, which came from the grinding. So the bread was gritty and wore away the Egyptians' teeth! The flour was mixed with water and baked in ovens.

BEER
Beer was made from partly baked barley bread, barley, and water. This was mashed up together, left for a few days, and then strained into beer jars. It was still thick and lumpy and had to be drunk through a wooden strainer (like a thick straw)!

A closer view of a **granary**. You can see the different bins for the different kinds of grain. Servants are collecting grain, and it is being measured out and recorded. Women are husking and grinding corn in the yard.

Owning animals was a sign of wealth in Ancient Egypt. Animals were also killed in **religious ceremonies** for the gods. There were ordinary uses for animals, too.

Cattle were used to pull the **plows**, but most animals were raised as food. Cows, sheep, and goats were kept for milk and meat. Animal skins were used for clothes and sandals. Ducks and geese were kept for eggs and meat. Fish were often kept in the duck ponds. Bees were kept in hives for honey to sweeten food and drink.

This model is from the tomb of an important Egyptian, Chancellor Meketer. It shows Meketer watching his cattle being counted.

20

COUNTING ANIMALS

Every year or two, all the animals on an **estate** were caught and counted—not just the cows and goats, but the ducks and geese too. The owner of the estate sat and watched as all of the animals were driven past. The work could take days.

Scribes wrote down how many animals there were. **Herdsmen** who had cared for their animals well were rewarded. Those who had not were punished. Then the animals were divided: some were kept and some were killed.

HUNTING FOR FOOD

The Ancient Egyptians hunted birds and fish on the river for food. Fishermen made a living catching fish. Some people made a living hunting wild birds for rich people to eat. Rich people went hunting for fun when they felt like it. **Tomb paintings** show the river and marshes full of birds and fish. Tomb paintings had to show life as being perfect so that the dead person's **afterlife** was perfect too!

THIS POEM, FROM ABOUT 2000 B.C., DESCRIBES A DAY'S HUNTING:

We go down to the marsh to trap birds and catch fish. It is a happy day. The marsh goddess is good to us. I make a screen for myself from the sun and settle on the riverbank. There are so many fish that my spear for catching them is never still. We get our bird nets ready. We pull the ropes when we hear them quack on the lake.

Wild birds were caught in a net and then prepared for cooking or storing.

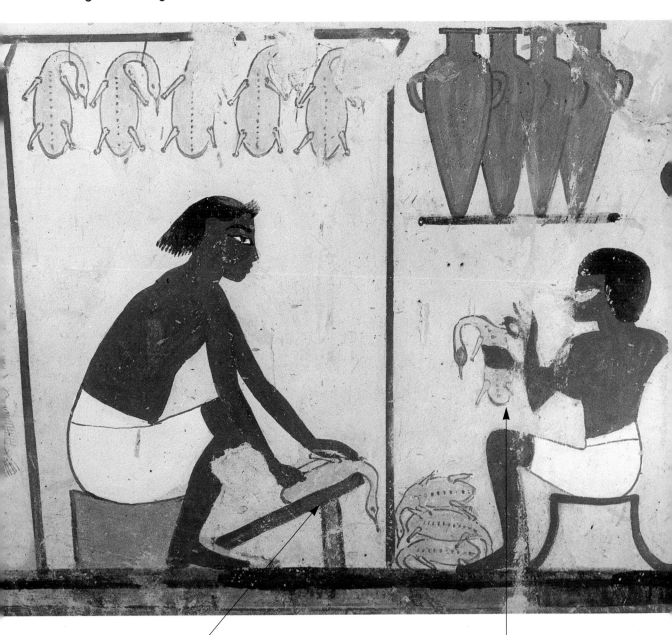

The plucked ducks then had their insides taken out and were hung in the sun to dry.

The feathers were plucked off the ducks while they were still warm.

VEGETABLES

Most ordinary Ancient Egyptians could not very often afford to buy meat or fish to eat. They lived mostly on bread, beer, and vegetables. They grew many different vegetables including onions, leeks, cabbages, lettuce, cucumbers, and different kinds of beans.

VEGETABLES AND HERBS WERE MORE THAN JUST FOOD. THEY WERE USED BY DOCTORS AS MEDICINE. THIS IS PART OF A BOOK OF MEDICAL CURES WRITTEN IN ABOUT 1500 B.C. THE EGYPTIANS BELIEVED THAT MANY ILLNESSES WERE CAUSED BY BLOOD AND OTHER LIQUIDS GETTING BLOCKED IN THE BODY.

If there is a blockage in the arm, you must give the patient fish and beer until he vomits. This clears the blockage. Then bandage his fingers with melon.

If the bowel is blocked, give the patient four pills made by mixing cucumber, senna, and sycamore seeds to a paste.

Grapes were eaten as fruit and made into wine. Here, workers are picking grapes and stomping them to make juice. The juice was collected as it came out of the spout on the right. It was then strained into wine jars.

FRUIT

The Egyptians planted fruit trees in gardens and along paths and rivers, as well as in orchards. Dates, figs, pomegranates, and grapes all grew well in the hot weather.

ORDINARY MEALS

Most cooking was done outside. Ovens were built in the yards of houses where the **grain** was stored. Bread was baked in the ovens. Most of the other food was cooked over an open fire. Ordinary people often cooked and ate their meals on the roofs of their houses, protected from the sun by a linen sheet on poles. People ate their main meal in the cool evening. They ate bread, vegetables, cheese, and fruit. They ate salted and fresh fish, but not a lot of meat. They drank beer or milk.

FEASTING

Rich people often ate outside. They ate the same things as ordinary people, but had meat more often and drank wine as well as beer. **Feast** times were different. It was important to have a lot to eat and drink. People ate vegetables cooked in different ways. They ate beef, goat, lamb, and all kinds of birds. On very special days, they might eat unusual meat like ostrich or giraffe.

A feast in an important home. The servants are serving, the guests are eating, the dancers are dancing, and the musicians are playing.

HOW DO WE KNOW WHAT THEY ATE?

EVIDENCE FROM THE TIME

We know what food the Ancient Egyptians ate because some **tomb paintings** show people eating or growing food. **Tomb models** also show people cooking. We even have food from the time that has been preserved in tombs.

GROWING FOOD

Tomb paintings and models show us how Egyptian farmers grew food. Some farming tools have survived too. The tools were made from wood. Egyptian farmers use similar methods today, although their tools are more modern.

This food was left for the dead in their tomb. There is bread, chicken, salted fish, and fruit.

NEW EVIDENCE

Archaeologists have studied the food from Ancient Egypt. They have studied the bodies of Ancient Egyptians. This has told them about the food these people ate. They found stone grit and sand in the bread and realized that this explained why Ancient Egyptians' teeth were so worn down.

This tomb painting shows the pond in the garden of a rich Egyptian. The pond is full of fish. Trees grow around the edges.

NEW MEDICINE?

A study of the ways herbs and food were used in medicine shows that some Ancient Egyptian herbal cures are very similar to cures used today.

- Senna is still used to clear out people's bowels.
- The Ancient Egyptians chewed willow leaves to stop pain. Scientists have studied willow leaves and found that they make a chemical very similar to that in aspirin (which is used today to stop pain).

afterlife the place where the Ancient Egyptians believed the dead lived

archaeologists people who dig up and study things left behind from past times

arura a piece of land that was big enough to grow enough food to feed a family for a year (about three-quarters of an acre)

corvée all Ancient Egyptians who were not **scribes** had to do this work on the **pharaoh's** land for a set number of days each year

crops plants that farmers grow for food or to use in other ways (to make clothes, baskets, or paper)

desert a dry place that has little or no rain all year

ditch a long and narrow hole dug out around a piece of land to trap water draining off it or to take water to it

estate a large piece of land with homes and farmland all run by the same person

feast a special meal with many different things to eat and drink. Feasts often celebrate special days.

grain types of grasses with fat seeds that are eaten. Barley, wheat, rye, oats, and rice are all grains.

granaries special places where **grain** is stored to keep it dry and to keep wild animals, such as mice, from eating it

ground crushing grain up until it is a powder (flour) and not seeds anymore

harvest to cut down, collect, and store **crops** that are ready to eat

herdsmen people who look after many animals that are kept together

husk the outside skin of a single piece of **grain**

inundation the time when the Nile River flooded and all the fields were under water

mummies bodies of dead people that have been preserved

oxen a type of cattle (cows and bulls)

pharaoh the king who ruled Egypt

plow a tool that turns over the soil to break it up

religious ceremonies special times when people go to one place to pray to a god or goddess

scribes the only people in Ancient Egypt who could read and write. Scribes ran the country for the **pharaoh.**

sluice a board across a ditch that can be lifted or closed to let water out or hold it in

starvation not having enough to eat

tax a payment that you have to make to whomever is running the country

temple a place where gods and goddesses are worshiped

tomb a place where someone is buried

tomb models tiny carvings or pottery shapes of people and things that were put in **tombs**

tomb paintings paintings on the walls of **tombs**

INDEX

MORE BOOKS TO READ

Balkwill, Richard. *Food & Feasts in Ancient Egypt.* Morristown, NJ: Silver Burdett Press. 1994.

Harris, Nathaniel. *Everyday Life in Ancient Egypt.* Danbury, CT: Franklin Watts, Inc. 1994

Kerr, Daisy. *Ancient Egyptians.* Danbury, CT: Franklin Watts, Inc. 1996.

Morley, Jaqueline. *How Would You Survive As an Ancient Egyptian?* Danbury, CT: Franklin Watts, Inc. 1995.

Wroble, Lisa A. *Kids in Ancient Egypt.* New York: Rosen Publishing Group. 1998.